The Dartmoor Pony

by Tracey Elliot-Reep

This book is dedicated to my mother, Elizabeth, who has devoted her life to Dartmoor ponies, through the Shilstone Rocks Stud. Also for her work and involvement with the Dartmoor Pony Moorland Scheme and the Dartmoor Pony Heritage Trust to ensure the ponies survival on the moor for future generations. I'd like to thank her for my childhood with these wonderful ponies and for passing her passion on to me.

Designed and published by Tracey Elliot-Reep 2014
Photographs and sketches © Tracey Elliot-Reep
Shilstone Rocks, Widecombe-in-the-Moor
Dartmoor, England

ISBN 978-1-905162-29-1

Thanks to
Jonathan Constant for his invaluable editing
Marian Constant for her advice and support

Dartmoor covers an area of 368 sq miles (954 sq km), making it the largest and wildest area of open country in the south west of England. It is one of the 15 National Parks of England, Wales and Scotland composed largely of granite, which is very evident on its numerous tors. The Dartmoor pony is the emblem of the Dartmoor National Park Authority (DNPA) and for many it is associated with the National Park.

The ponies on Dartmoor are an integral part of the landscape and many visitors to the National Park come specifically to see these animals in their natural environment. The healthy survival of the Dartmoor pony on the moor is in the minds of many people whose lives are touched by their presence.

Ponies have roamed Dartmoor for thousands of years. Approximately 3,500 years ago, the horse became common in Europe. The earliest evidence of ponies' hoof prints, dating back to 2000 BC, was found during excavations on south west Dartmoor in the 1970s. More recent archaeological finds elsewhere in the country suggest that horses, similar in size to the Dartmoor pony, pulled Roman chariots.

Some farmers put reflective collars around the ponies' necks (as above) which illuminate in car headlights.

The first written record of ponies on Dartmoor occurs in 1012, with reference to the 'wild horses' of Ashburton, owned by the Bishop of Crediton. Three 'unbroken' mares are mentioned in the Domesday Book entry for Cornwood (1086). In 1535, in an attempt to improve horses throughout the country, Henry VIII decreed that stallions under 13 hands high should not be used for breeding (fine 40 shillings), but the remote hill ponies seemed to escape the edict. Early manorial records indicate that, as today, many ponies remained unbroken, but all were branded and usually ear-marked.

Early tin workers used them as pack ponies to bring tin ingots off the moor to be assayed (weighed and valued) at the 'stannary' towns of Ashburton, Tavistock, Chagford and Plympton. After the tin mining era, while some ponies were left to roam free on the moor, others were used for work on the farms, mainly for shepherding and as driving ponies to take the family to market and to church.

Over the centuries, a variety of stallions have been raised on Dartmoor depending on the demand at the time. When pack ponies were required, the native ponies were crossed with roadsters – a bigger breed. When there was demand for polo ponies, thoroughbreds, Arabs, Fells and New Forest were used. In the coal-mining era, Shetlands were brought down from the north and crossed with Dartmoor ponies to produce smaller ponies to pull wagons from the coalface. Some of these were stabled underground and after their arrival at the pit, they never again saw the light of day.

Haytor Rocks

Ponies were also used to pull wagons above ground on Dartmoor. In the mid 1800s, Dartmoor was the main source of granite in Britain – at Haytor there are the remains of a stone railway, used to transport granite to the quayside at Teigngrace and then on to the coast by canal. Old London Bridge was built from Haytor granite.

Ernie Worth (above) used to milk his cows, and for 40 years he and his pony did a delivery round in Princetown. This same pony was used in the afternoon to round up sheep, pull the hay cutters and then get the hay into ricks, using wooden sweeps, at Peat Cott and Castle Farm.

In medieval times the most common method of transporting goods across Dartmoor was the packhorse, which used to cross the many rivers on the moor via clapper bridges similar to this one at Postbridge.

The Dartmoor pony has a very kind nature and is an ideal pony for children. With their careful movement they are wonderful schoolmasters for young children and also make excellent Pony Club mounts and driving ponies, as they are level headed, able and willing. Having strong build, limbs and bone they can also carry a small adult quite easily.

They make excellent ponies for in-hand showing, lead rein, first ridden, open ridden, working hunter, hunter trails, dressage, pony club, hunting and cross country, and they go well in harness, making them very smart driving ponies.

The small, tough and sure-footed Dartmoor Pony provided excellent foundation stock for polo ponies, which became a popular sport in the latter half of the 19th century, when army officers returned from India where it originated. In 1917, the Prince of Wales founded the Duchy Stud at Tor Royal (near Princetown) to breed suitable ponies for the game.

In 1893, the National Pony Society was formed, and laid down standards for each of the nine native pony breeds of the United Kingdom. The Dartmoor Pony Society was formed in 1925 and has continued to ensure the quality of this registered rare breed and to preserve the indigenous pony both on and off the moor. Dartmoors have been exported worldwide, including Australia, Austria, Canada, Denmark, the Falkland Islands, France, Germany, Holland, Malta, New Zealand, Norway, Sweden, Switzerland, the United Arab Emirates and the USA. Many of these countries have thriving Dartmoor Pony Societies.

The purebred registered Dartmoor pony

Breed Standard of the Dartmoor Pony

Height: not exceeding 12.2 hands high (127cms)

Colour: bay, brown, black, grey, chestnut, roan. Piebalds and skewbalds are not allowed. Excessive white markings are discouraged.

Head and neck: the head should be small with large kindly eyes and small alert ears. It should be well set on a good neck of medium length. The throat and jaws should be fine and showing no signs of coarseness or throatiness.

Stallions have a moderate crest.

Shoulders: good shoulders are most important. They should be well laid back and sloping, but not too fine at the withers.

Loins: neither level nor steeply sloping. The tail is well set up.

Limbs: the hocks should be well let down with plenty of length from hip to hock, clean cut with plenty of bone below the hock. They should have a strong second thigh. They should not be 'sickled' or 'cow-hocked'. The forelegs should not be tied in at the knee. The forearm should be muscular and relatively long and the knee fairly large and flat at the front. The cannons should be short with ample good, flat, flinty bone. The pasterns should be sloping but not too long. The feet should be hard and well shaped.

Movement: low and straight coming from the shoulder with good hock action but without exaggeration.

General: the mane and tail should be full and flowing.

The Dartmoor is a very good-looking riding pony, sturdily built yet with quality.

Dartmoor pony stallion

Dartmoor pony mare

Dartmoor pony ridden under saddle

Dartmoor pony yearling colt

The Dartmoor Pony Society represents the pedigree Dartmoor pony (with known breeding), and is the breed's guardian on Dartmoor and the mother society of the breed worldwide. Such is the relative rarity of the Dartmoor Pony today, that it is listed by the Rare Breeds Survival Trust.

There are many ponies living on Dartmoor, of all sizes and colours, but these are mostly of unknown breeding. The true-to-type Dartmoor ponies, with known breeding, are recognised and appear in show rings at county shows throughout the United Kingdom.

The primary role of the Society is to maintain the Stud Book, which holds records tracing the pedigrees of the registered Dartmoor pony over 100 years.

Coloured part-bred cross

Pedigree Dartmoor stallion

The multi-coloured ponies are crosses with other breeds

Shetland ponies

The ponies seen grazing on the moor are not all Dartmoor ponies, but vary widely – from the registered pure bred that may win at The Horse of the Year Show, to cross breeds and the Shetland crosses, which can have many patterns on their coats. In between are the traditional moorland ponies that some farmers have bred true to type for generations.

Above: Traditional type ponies. The colours of the traditional and pure bred Dartmoor pony range from brown, black, grey (white), chestnut to roan. Piebalds (black and white) and skewbalds (brown and white) are crossbreds, often part Shetland.

Next page: Pure bred pedigree ponies living out on Dartmoor in the winter.

Foaling Time

Most foals are born between April and July. Mares will carry their foals for an average of 333 days (just over 11 months) although fillies tend to be born a day or two before colts. During the last three months before foaling, the body weight of the foal foetus increases by two-thirds.

The foal starts breathing when the navel is parted and the oxygen and nutrition from the mother ceases. The mare will lick the mucus off its coat, conscientiously from head to feet, and rub it with her muzzle, which stimulates the circulation and helps the coat to dry. She then pushes her foal to and fro to encourage it to stand up, and shortly it will instinctively find its way to the udder to drink the important colostrum (first) milk.

Spring foals!

The foal's body weight doubles in the first couple of months and it grows 80% of its height in its first year. With the flush of spring grass in the valley pastures, the ponies exchange their thick winter coats for sleek shiny ones. The newborn foal's coat is quite fluffy until the second month when a smoother summer coat grows.

Shilstone Rocks Herd

The foals enjoy the spring and summer with their mothers and are usually weaned at five or six months.

Emsworthy and Hound Tor

Funny faces!

The Dartmoor Pony Moorland Scheme

In the late 1980s, the Duchy of Cornwall set out to improve the quality and type of the Dartmoor pony by demonstrating good selection and management. Together with the Dartmoor Pony Society and the Dartmoor National Park Authority, it created the Dartmoor Pony Moorland Scheme.

Each spring, owners of suitable mares living on Dartmoor are invited to put them in a moorland enclosure (known as a 'newtake') with pedigree stallions, and here they remain throughout the summer months. The young ponies bred in the newtakes spend the winters on less exposed sites – they often play a vital role through 'conservation grazing' on land owned by organisations such as the National Trust, helping to encourage the return of rare wild flowers, plants and the virtually extinct large blue butterfly.

All breeding mares are inspected by the Dartmoor Pony Society's inspectors and are branded if accepted. They are admitted to the newtakes free of charge, and a payment is made to their owners to help them with management costs.

A difficult economic climate and increasing regulations have led to a fall in demand for ponies. The Dartmoor Pony Moorland Scheme responded by reducing the number of foals bred in recent years, and also introduced a non-breeding newtake, which offers cost-effective seasonal grazing. It remains dedicated to preserving the ponies and their bloodlines, so that Dartmoor can continue to be blessed by the sight of traditional ponies for generations to come.

All foals bred from the scheme must be inspected and, if approved, they are recorded in the Dartmoor Pony Society supplementary register. A fourth generation foal is eligible for pedigree registration. The Scheme continues to be successful in producing top quality foals, many of which have gone on to win local and national shows.

Ponies are uniquely suited to life on the moor, whose gorse and brambles form an important part of their diet, especially in winter. They are also great conservationists – by trampling old gorse and grasses, the ponies allow more light to reach the ground, encouraging sensitive plants to grow and preventing the moor from becoming an impenetrable forest.

Traditonal type Dartmoor ponies on Bonehill Down.

Dartmoor stallion Shilstone Rocks Snowgoose

Dartmoor pony stallions have excellent temperaments. After an initial play fight when they were first turned out together, these stallions at Shilstone Rocks stud, Widecombe-in-the-Moor, were happy to run together – proof of their kind nature.

Above: Looking towards Haytor from Seven Lord's Land.

Top left: Chagford Common, looking towards Birch Tor and Hameldown. Middle: Holwell and (below) Chagford Common.

Farmers have grazing rights on different commons on Dartmoor. The ponies possess a natural homing instinct to their patch, even when there are no walls to confine them, and know their own territory by instinct – described locally as 'leared'.

Drifting across Widecombe hill

Autumn Drift

In late September and early October, local farmers who have grazing rights and keep ponies on the moor will head out onto their area of common to round the animals up – a process known as 'drifting'. On foot, or mounted on horses or quad bikes, they herd the ponies into small enclosures or yards, where they are sorted into groups according to ownership.

    After drifting the ponies, the farmers decide which ones to sell, and return the rest to the moor until the following year. A few foals will go back on the moor, some may become children's ponies or even be used for carriage driving, but the majority of foals and old mares will end up as meat for the local zoo.

There are three groups dedicated to ponies on Dartmoor. The Dartmoor Pony Society is the guardian of pedigree Dartmoor ponies and is also involved with the Duchy Newtake Scheme, which seeks to improve the quality of the breed.

The Dartmoor Pony Heritage Trust's mission is to protect the indigenous Dartmoor Pony from extinction and to maintain its presence on Dartmoor – preserving this precious heritage for future generations. The Dartmoor Hill Pony Association supports all ponies, including crossbreds and coloured ponies, on the Dartmoor commons. (See inside back cover for websites.)

The ponies on the moor face a bleak and uncertain future as a result of increased EU regulations and the added cost of 'passports' and micro chipping, which is not covered by the price the farmers get from the sale of their ponies. Several farmers have recently got rid of all their ponies, as they are no longer financially viable. Some people believe the way forward is to control the quality and quantity of stallions allowed to run on the moor.

The Dartmoor Pony Heritage Trust offers an adoption programme for foals coming off the moor. After filming the last autumn drift, I adopted two fillies into the Heritage Scheme and named them Dunstone Wittaborough and Dunstone Pudsham after the herd and area in which they would have been born.

The Heritage Trust organised their 'passports' and micro chipping and after spending several days being handled, they wintered down on the edge of Dartmoor and came back in the spring to be handled again. Later they will probably go on to graze a large area of moorland that the DPHT leases from the Forestry Commission at Bellever, in the heart of the moor.
At its centre at Parke, the DPHT uses some of the ponies in educational, motivational and emotional development activities, helping disadvantaged young people develop life skills through the training of unhandled and handled foals and ponies.

54

The ponies which are drifted off the Widecombe commons are sorted by ownership at Great Dunstone farm.

Autumn mists are created when the temperature changes, and can be spectacular on Dartmoor. Once the mares are returned to the moor, mostly without their foals, they will continue to graze their area until the following autumn drift.

Winters are long and harsh, so the ponies need to be hardy. Continuous rain has more of an effect on them than snow, as the water soaks through their thick coats. The ponies forage for grass almost continually throughout the day, although on some sunny mornings they will stop and even lie down to sunbathe, soaking up the warmth of the sun.

View from Pil Tor towards Holne Moor.

Stallions enjoying a roll and play in the winter sunshine, on the Shilstone Rocks stud above Widecombe-in-the-Moor

Ponies are often seen wandering around Widecombe Green, through the village and along the lanes, foraging for grass.

Photographer then and now! Tracey Elliot-Reep with her ponies Shilstone Rocks Rainstorm and Rainbow and (below) as a child, with Shilstone Rocks Windswept I.

Photographer Tracey Elliot-Reep

Tracey Elliot-Reep was born on Dartmoor and grew up at her mother's Shilstone Rocks Dartmoor pony stud, in Widecombe-in-the-Moor. Here's a bit of her story;

"My lifelong love of Dartmoor ponies was inspired by my mother's passion for breeding them at Shilstone Rocks, our family home. I had dyslexia and continually struggled at school, but my happiest childhood memories always involve ponies. On our one and only family holiday, we camped in a horsebox above Sennen Cove in Cornwall, and I rode bareback, sliding down the sand dunes and racing across the beach. On my seventh birthday, my father led a bay Dartmoor pony into the kitchen, wrapped in brown paper! His name was Little Goose, and he had black points and a big star on his forehead. I remember walking back from school and taking bridles to the field to catch Little Goose for myself and another pony for a friend. We didn't bother with saddles. We just jumped on bareback and raced around the lanes and over the moor, playing cowboys and Indians – a dream that was realised decades later when I rode Quarter horses from Mexico to Canada!"

Rainbow in her early days

Sire Shilstone Rocks North Countryman (above) in a blizzard and having a roll!

Shilstone Rocks Mountain Bay, and (right) all rugged up, looking like a pantomine horse!

Dartmoor ponies to New Zealand

"I have a dream to set up ranches and farms around the world to help children who need healing – whether spiritually, emotionally or physically – while at the same time helping to ensure the survival of the breed, which is ideally suited to young handlers and riders. I recently started to put my dream into action by exporting two Shilstone Rocks Dartmoor mares to New Zealand. Their names are Shilstone Rocks Mountain Bay and Shilstone Rocks Sugar Snap, and they were given to me and my sister (who lives in New Zealand) by my mother. Before they left, in the depths of the British winter, we put them in foal to Shilstone Rocks North Countryman."

"The flight and the extensive vet checks made the journey to New Zealand both complex and expensive, especially since I'd decided to put them in foal. On the other hand, it meant I was flying four for the price of two! After clipping them out (they were flying from winter to summer) they spent three weeks in quarantine in England and another three weeks in New Zealand."

Photo by Bridget McCormick

"In October (spring in New Zealand), Mountain Bay had a bay colt, who we called Mountain Man, and Sugar Snap had a bay filly, who we called Snowberry (she was conceived in the snow on Dartmoor!). Both bear a strong resemblance to their sire, Shilstone Rocks North Countryman. Hawkes Bay is a stark contrast to Dartmoor, but Sugar Snap (below right) is still a good conservationist, eating thistle weeds!

Shilstone Rocks Mountain Bay, Sugar Snap, Snowberry and Mountain Man on Waitomo Farm in Hawkes Bay, New Zealand.

Ponies have roamed Dartmoor for thousands of years, but they now they face an uncertain future. Thankfully, there are dedicated organisations and individuals who share a determination to conserve these ponies, so that future generations can enjoy seeing them in their natural habitat.